YOU'LL NEVER WALK ALONE

LIVERPOOL
FOOTBALL CLUB

EST·1892 ®

THE OFFICIAL
LIVERPOOL FC
ANNUAL 2014

Written by Mark Platt

Designed by Brian Thomson

A Grange Publication

© 2013. Published by Grange Communications Ltd., Edinburgh, under licence from The Liverpool Football Club and Athletic Grounds Ltd. Printed in the EU.

ISBN 978-1-908925-44-2

£7.99

Liverpool Football Club Honours Board

1976

*European Cup/UEFA Champions
League Winners*
1977, 1978, 1981, 1984, 2005

First Division Champions
1900/01, 1905/06, 1921/22, 1922/23,
1946/47, 1963/64, 1965/66, 1972/73,
1975/76, 1976/77, 1978/79, 1979/80,
1981/82, 1982/83, 1983/84, 1985/86,
1987/88, 1989/90

FA Cup Winners
1965, 1974, 1986, 1989, 1992, 2001, 2006

UEFA Cup Winners
1973, 1976, 2001

League Cup Winners
1981, 1982, 1983, 1984, 1995, 2001,
2003, 2012

Second Division Champions
1893/94, 1895/96, 1904/05, 1961/62

European Super Cup/UEFA Super Cup Winners
1977, 2001, 2005

ScreenSport Super Cup Winners
1985/86

Charity/Community Shield Winners
1964*, 1965*, 1966, 1974, 1976, 1977*,
1979, 1980, 1982, 1986*, 1988, 1989,
1990*, 2001, 2006 (*shared)

FA Youth Cup Winners
1995/96, 2005/06, 2006/07

Reserve League Champions
1956/57, 1968/69, 1969/70, 1970/71,
1972/73, 1973/74, 1974/75, 1975/76,
1976/77, 1978/79, 1979/80, 1980/81,
1981/82, 1983/84, 1984/85, 1989/90,
1999/2000, 2007/08

1977

1980

1974

1984

1986

1990

2005

2012

YOU'LL NEVER WALK ALONE

LIVERPOOL
FOOTBALL CLUB

EST·1892 ®

Contents

SEASON REVIEW

AUGUST 2012

With Brendan Rodgers taking charge of his first competitive games, August marked the dawn of a new era at Anfield, but it was with a mixed bag of results that Liverpool opened the 2012/13 season. Summer signing Fabio Borini was quick off the mark as the Reds cruised past FC Gomel of Belarus in the 3rd qualifying round of the Europa League and a place in the group phase was then secured at the expense of Heart of Midlothian in an intriguing all-British play-off tie. Unfortunately, the pleasing European form went out the window when Liverpool kicked off their FA Barclays Premier League campaign. A crushing 3-0 defeat by West Bromwich Albion on a baking hot day in the Midlands put an instant dampener on any pre-season optimism, although pride was temporarily restored the following week with a creditable 2-2 draw at home to reigning champions, Manchester City – a game in which Liverpool twice led and would have won had Carlos Tevez not taken advantage of an unfortunate back-pass by Martin Skrtel, ten minutes from time.

2/8/12	Gomel	(a)	Europa League 3rd Qualifying round	1-0
9/8/12	Gomel	(h)	Europa League 3rd Qualifying round	3-0
18/8/12	West Bromwich Albion	(a)	FA Barclays Premier League	0-3
23/8/12	Hearts	(a)	Europa League Play-off	1-0
26/8/12	Manchester City	(h)	FA Barclays Premier League	2-2
30/8/12	Hearts	(h)	Europa League Play-off	1-1

2/9/12	Arsenal	(h)	FA Barclays Premier League	0-2
15/9/12	Sunderland	(a)	FA Barclays Premier League	1-1
20/9/12	Young Boys	(a)	Europa League Group Phase	5-3
23/9/12	Manchester United	(h)	FA Barclays Premier League	1-2
26/9/12	West Bromwich Albion	(a)	Capital One Cup 3rd round	2-1
29/9/12	Norwich City	(a)	FA Barclays Premier League	5-2

SEPTEMBER 2012

A second successive Carrow Road hat-trick for Luis
Suarez, and first Premier League win of the season,
was the highlight of a month that saw Liverpool once
again plagued by inconsistency, with disappointing
home defeats to Arsenal and Manchester United the
major low-points. In the Europa League Brendan
Rodgers was rewarded for rotating his squad and
fielding four debutants with a thrilling 5-3 victory
over Young Boys in Berne, while the Reds began their
defence of the newly rebranded Capital One Cup
by avenging their early season loss at West Brom
on what was a landmark night at The Hawthorns.
Midfielder Nuri Sahin, a recent loan acquisition from
Real Madrid, netted his first goals for the club in a
2-1 win, while debutant Jerome Sinclair made history
by becoming the club's youngest ever player at just
16 years and six days old.

OCTOBER 2012

An incident-packed Goodison derby ended in controversy with legitimate claims that the visitors should have been making the short journey back across Stanley Park with all three points. Luis Suarez fired Liverpool into an early two-goal lead but Everton drew level before the break. However, Suarez looked to have dramatically won the game in injury time only for the goal to be wrongly ruled out for offside. Earlier in the month, Liverpudlians finally got to cheer a home win in the league when Raheem Sterling's first senior goal gave the Reds all three points against Reading, but October finished disappointingly as eventual winners Swansea ended Liverpool's interest in the Capital One Cup with an impressive 3-1 win in front of the Kop.

4/10/12	Udinese	(h)	Europa League Group Phase	2-3
7/10/12	Stoke City	(h)	FA Barclays Premier League	0-0
20/10/12	Reading	(h)	FA Barclays Premier League	1-0
25/10/12	Anzhi	(h)	Europa League Group Phase	1-0
28/10/12	Everton	(a)	FA Barclays Premier League	2-2
31/10/12	Swansea City	(h)	Capital One Cup 4th round	1-3

NOVEMBER 2012

A creditable 1-1 draw away to the reigning European Champions and an impressive performance at home to Wigan were the stand-out moments of a month that saw Luis Suarez once again take the personal plaudits. The Uruguayan netted four times in November including a goal of the season contender that rescued a point at home to Newcastle. In the Europa League, an away defeat to Anzhi and a draw at home to Young Boys left our hopes of qualification teetering on the brink.

4/11/12	Newcastle United	(h)	FA Barclays Premier League	1-1
8/11/12	Anzhi	(a)	Europa League Group Phase	0-1
11/11/12	Chelsea	(a)	FA Barclays Premier League	1-1
17/11/12	Wigan Athletic	(h)	FA Barclays Premier League	3-0
22/11/12	Young Boys	(h)	Europa League Group Phase	2-2
25/11/12	Swansea City	(a)	FA Barclays Premier League	0-0
28/11/12	Tottenham Hotspur	(a)	FA Barclays Premier League	1-2

DECEMBER 2012

For the first time in the season Liverpool recorded back-to-back victories in the Premier League, while Jordan Henderson's solitary strike away to Udinese was enough to clinch qualification to the knockout phase of the Europa League. But just when it looked as though the Reds had finally turned the corner, a shock home defeat against struggling Aston Villa brought everyone crashing back down to earth. Emphatic wins over Fulham and Queens Park Rangers either side of Christmas lifted spirits but a Boxing Day battering at Stoke served as a stark reminder that further improvement was required.

1/12/12	Southampton	(h)	FA Barclays Premier League	1-0
6/12/12	Udinese	(a)	FA Barclays Premier League	1-0
9/12/12	West Ham United	(a)	FA Barclays Premier League	3-2
15/12/12	Aston Villa	(h)	FA Barclays Premier League	1-3
22/12/12	Fulham	(h)	FA Barclays Premier League	4-0
26/12/12	Stoke City	(a)	FA Barclays Premier League	1-3
30/12/12	Queens Park Rangers	(a)	FA Barclays Premier League	3-0

JANUARY 2013

The New Year brought two new recruits and fresh hope, yet still some of the same old problems persisted. Daniel Sturridge celebrated his arrival from Chelsea with the opening goal of the FA Cup third round win at non-league Mansfield Town, and he was on target again the following week in a narrow defeat at Old Trafford, while the signing of Philippe Coutinho from Inter Milan late in the month was viewed as a coup. But just eight days after producing what was arguably their best performance of the season to date, in the 5-0 rout of Norwich, the dark clouds began to hover once more as the Reds found themselves on the wrong end of a major FA Cup giant-killing away to League One Oldham. Four nights later, despite a much-improved performance, a two-goal lead was surrendered at Arsenal and Liverpool remained seventh in the table, with hopes of a top four finish looking more and more forlorn.

2/1/13	Sunderland	(h)	FA Barclays Premier League	3-0
6/1/13	Mansfield Town	(a)	FA Cup 3rd round	2-1
13/1/13	Manchester United	(a)	FA Barclays Premier League	1-2
19/1/13	Norwich City	(h)	FA Barclays Premier League	5-0
27/1/13	Oldham Athletic	(a)	FA Cup 4th round	2-3
30/1/13	Arsenal	(a)	FA Barclays Premier League	2-2

FEBRUARY 2013

Another month of contrasting emotions began with more hard luck against the champions. Goals from Daniel Sturridge and Steven Gerrard saw Liverpool come from behind and seemingly on course for a morale-boosting victory at the Etihad, until a rare Pepe Reina error gifted Manchester City an undeserved equaliser. Philippe Coutinho netted his first goal for the club in a 5-0 win over a Swansea team that would soon succeed Liverpool as League Cup winners, while veteran defender Jamie Carragher announced that he would be hanging up his boots come the end of the season. He played his final European game for the club when Liverpool failed to overturn a 2-0 first-leg deficit against Zenit St Petersburg in the Europa League round of 32.

3/2/13	Manchester City	(a)	FA Barclays Premier League	2-2
11/2/13	West Bromwich Albion	(h)	FA Barclays Premier League	0-2
14/2/13	Zenit St Petersburg	(a)	Europa League round of 32	0-2
17/2/13	Swansea City	(h)	FA Barclays Premier League	5-0
21/2/13	Zenit St Petersburg	(h)	Europa League round of 32	3-1

MARCH 2013

Free to concentrate on the league, the Reds threatened to hit top form in March and began the month in some style. The increasingly impressive Philippe Coutinho linked up superbly with Luis Suarez to inspire a 4-0 drubbing of Wigan at the DW Stadium, while a late Steven Gerrard penalty clinched a five-goal thriller at home to Champions League-chasing Tottenham. It was the only time Liverpool would beat a team above them in the league that season. Unfortunately, the momentum couldn't be maintained and Liverpool were made to pay for an off-day on the South Coast as lowly Southampton brought the winning run to an abrupt end, though hopes of European qualification were kept alive by an Easter Sunday away-win over Aston Villa.

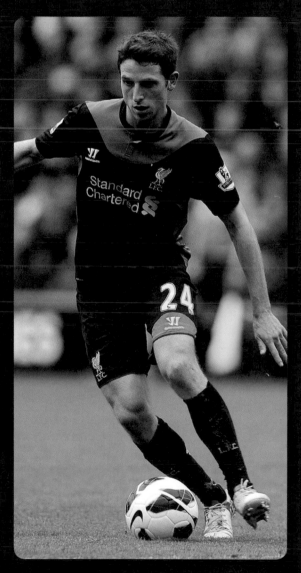

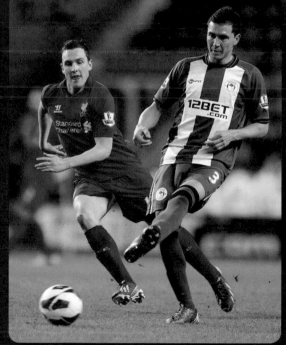

2/3/13	Wigan Athletic	(a)	FA Barclays Premier League	4-0
10/3/13	Tottenham Hotspur	(h)	FA Barclays Premier League	3-2
16/3/13	Southampton	(a)	FA Barclays Premier League	1-3
31/3/13	Aston Villa	(a)	FA Barclays Premier League	2-1

APRIL 2013

Off the pitch, Anfield once again fell silent on April 15th as the victims of Hillsborough were remembered on the 24th anniversary of the tragedy. On it, three successive draws all but quashed Liverpool's hopes of jumping ahead of Everton and challenging for the Premier League's final European place. The headlines in the latter part of this month though were dominated by Luis Suarez. The Reds number seven netted his 30th goal of the season to steal a late point in the 2-2 home draw with Chelsea but an earlier incident with Branislav Ivanovic was to result in him being slapped with the ten-game ban that brought his season to a sudden halt. Liverpool responded by brushing aside that controversy and romping to their biggest win of the season without him, scoring six goals without reply up at Newcastle to end April on a high.

7/4/13	West Ham United	(h)	FA Barclays Premier League	0-0
13/4/13	Reading	(a)	FA Barclays Premier League	0-0
21/4/13	Chelsea	(h)	FA Barclays Premier League	2-2
27/4/13	Newcastle United	(a)	FA Barclays Premier League	6-0

5/5/13	Everton	(h)	FA Barclays Premier League	0-0
12/5/13	Fulham	(a)	FA Barclays Premier League	3-1
19/5/13	Queens Park Rangers	(h)	FA Barclays Premier League	1-0

MAY 2013

Although Liverpool had nothing but pride to play for
as the 2012/13 campaign drew to a close, May was
a momentous month for veteran defender Jamie
Carragher who played his 737th and final game in
the 1-0 victory over Queens Park Rangers. Carragher
bowed out amid emotional scenes at Anfield on an
afternoon when a lone strike from Philippe Coutinho
ensured the Reds signed off in style. Earlier in the
month the 220th Merseyside derby had ended in
stalemate, while Daniel Sturridge registered his first
hat-trick in a Liverpool shirt, but May 2013 was all
about saying goodbye to a living legend.

Manager Profile

His first season in the Anfield hot-seat may have yielded no silverware but Liverpool manager Brendan Rodgers believes the 2012/13 campaign was a vitally important one in terms of progress towards a brighter future...

Brendan, how do you assess your first season at the club?

I've been satisfied; I think that's the best description. We had to make lots of changes and not just on the field. It took us a bit of time to get going with on-the-field performances but I believe as the season's gone on we've improved and developed. I maintain the overriding feeling that it's a privilege to be manager of this football club and hopefully I can do it justice as time goes on.

What were your main priorities when taking the job as Liverpool manager?

First and foremost I wanted to get to know the people – the football players and the staff. Liverpool as a football club has always been renowned as having good people. But you need to get to know them. The job for me wasn't just to build a team, it was to build a football club, and to look at the infrastructure, and see what we can develop and improve in order to build a stable base that would allow us to move forward. So that was the main criteria: assess the squad and assess the staff.

How would you describe the style of play and footballing philosophy you are trying to implement here?

The objective is to win, that is the most important factor of what we're trying to achieve in it all, but in every way there's a way of winning. For me, it was about protecting the philosophy and the reputation of this great club in terms of the way they were playing. The playing style has always been about attractive attacking football, but always with tactical discipline. We want to play the football in the opponent's half, we want to be as creative as we can, scoring as many goals as we can and making sure we have that tactical balance and discipline in the team, conceding as little as possible. What's also important is our pressing, our attitude and hunger to regain the ball – that's critical for us. Dominance with the ball will enable us to create chances but in order to have it you have to win it back quickly and that's something we do a lot of work on.

Are there any particular stand-out games for you that best illustrate this?

We had a number of good performances that I was pleased with. Like the one up at Newcastle for example, where the football was fluent, the goals flowed and we kept a clean sheet. I've got to say there were also a lot of the games where I felt our control, the speed of our game and our pressing and offensive play was very good, without us achieving the desired results – like at home to the two Manchester clubs. There were also a handful that didn't epitomise what we're trying to do, but that's natural. Our idea is to find consistency in that group, and that's something that we'll be constantly striving for.

And how excited are you about the January signing: Philippe Coutinho?

Philippe is another wonderful footballer. For someone so young he has real football intelligence and a mature head on his shoulders. It's hard to believe at times and you can only imagine what he's going to be like over the next few years. Next season is going to be a big one for him but he's a massive talent. He's adapted perfectly and I believe he will go on to be an outstanding player for Liverpool.

Has the scale of this job lived up to your expectations?

I've been around football for a long time. I've worked at big clubs, so I understand the scale of it, but you never know totally until you come in, and certainly coming into Liverpool this first season has been a remarkable journey. Because of the history at this club the expectancy is huge, and rightfully so, but I enjoy that. I enjoy the fact that it's a big challenge. There will never be a lazy day here; you can never afford to have one. The facts are simple. We finished 30 points behind the leaders, 12 points from the team in fourth and were not good enough in the cups. That is something we have to address. We want to be up there challenging in every competition. My job is to find the solutions, and deal with the expectancy, and that is something I'm committed to doing.

Are you confident of achieving that?

Yes, I am. My first season here was never going to be one in which we made giant strides. But we have taken steps in the right direction. I really do believe that. They may only be small steps but in terms of where we want to be heading they are important. It's all about finding the consistency needed to become realistic challengers and I'm very confident that we can continue to build on the progress already made.

Reds all over

UK

19.2% of all TVs in the UK were tuned in to the 2005 Champions League Final

SPAIN

14.8% of all TVs in Spain were tuned in to the 2005 Champions League Final

ITALY

20.1% of all TVs in Italy were tuned in to the 2005 Champions League Final

OVER 500m FOOTBALL FANS worldwide tuned in to see a recent Liverpool v Man United match at Anfield

OVER 200 OFFICIAL SUPPORTERS' CLUBS

IN 57 COUNTRIES

Liverpool Football Club has just over 200 Official Supporters' Clubs all over the world in 57 different countries. Our Official Supporters' Clubs provide a valuable service to loyal Liverpool Football Club supporters living in the local area. The Supporters' Clubs also provide an excellent way of meeting fellow supporters who are devoted to following Liverpool Football Club, wherever they live in the world.

Official Supporters' Clubs are closely affiliated to Liverpool Football Club and enjoy a close working relationship with the club. If you would like to contact your local Supporters' Club, please visit our website for more information:

www.liverpoolfc.com/fans/lfc-official-supporters-clubs

The estimated worldwide audience that watched the Champions League Final in 2005 was approx

73m

the world

YOU'LL NEVER WALK ALONE

LIVERPOOL
FOOTBALL CLUB

EST·1892

CROATIA

18.1%
of all TVs in Croatia
were tuned in to the
2005 Champions
League Final

OVER
388m
ASIAN FANS
follow the Reds

THAILAND

There are over 400,000
fans in Bangkok who
follow Liverpool on
Facebook. This is more
than double the amount
of any other city in
the world.

CHINA

There are more
Liverpool supporters
(over 1.5m) in China
than any other
country in the world.

TURKEY

19.8%
of all TVs in Turkey
were tuned in to the
2005 Champions
League Final

INDONESIA

Liverpool have more
Facebook followers in
Indonesia than any other
country in the world,
overtaking the UK for the
first time in January 2013.

OVER 588 MILLION FANS WORLDWIDE

AND COUNTING...

AUSTRALIA

The 95,000 plus sell-out
crowd that witnessed
Liverpool's historic match
at the MCG in July 2013
was the highest attendance
ever for a football fixture
in Australia and a new
record for that stadium.

CARRAGHER
Farewell to a Legend
Anfield waved goodbye to a club icon on 19 May 2013.

After 737 appearances – the second highest total in Liverpool history – Jamie Carragher bowed out amid emotional scenes on the final day of the FA Barclays Premier League season.

It brought the curtain down on a remarkable career in the Reds first team for Bootle-born Carragher.

With a glittering array of medals and enough magical memories to last a lifetime he will go down in Kop folklore as one of the club's greatest servants.

A graduate of Liverpool's old Centre of Excellence, Carra rose through the ranks and battled his way to the very top. At the peak of his game he was widely regarded as one of the finest defenders in Europe and his defensive heroics played a key role in Liverpool's many trophy triumphs of the noughties.

His unbridled passion for the game ensured he was also a cult-hero among the fans and while his final appearance in a red shirt was tinged with sadness for all those who sang about a 'Team of Carraghers', it was also a celebration of a remarkable career, the likes of which we may never see again.

Fact-file

BORN: Bootle, 28 January 1978

OTHER CLUBS: None

JOINED LIVERPOOL: 1987 (signed professional 1996)

DEBUT: 8 January 1997, Middlesbrough (a) lost 1-2

LAST APPEARANCE: 19 May 2013, Queens Park Rangers (h) won 1-0

INTERNATIONAL CAPS: 38 (England)

TOTAL APPEARANCES: 737

TOTAL GOALS: 5

Honours won:

- UEFA Champions League 2005
- FA Cup 2001, 2006
- UEFA Cup 2001
- League Cup 2001, 2003, 2012
- European Super Cup 2001, 2005
- Charity/Community Shield 2001, 2006
- FA Youth Cup 1996

To commemorate his retirement Jamie flicks through his photo album to tell us the story behind six of his most memorable snaps...

On the spot (above) 2001 Worthing Cup Final penalty shoot-out v Birmingham

I had no nerves, I've got to be honest. I put it right in the top corner and I think a lot of that was to do with the fact that I was very relaxed. I look back now and think about what it would be like to watch my son or someone I know going up to take the penalty, I'd be so nervous watching it. I just went up and took it and it went in. That was the first trophy that I won [the League Cup] so it was a special occasion.

Istanbul (below)

When I talk about my best moment in football, it would be that. I think that's a brilliant picture. It shows that realisation – we've just won the European Cup. Even Harry Kewell's running and he came off injured! You just can't beat pictures like that. You just look at the facial expressions and it's the same for everyone. I just think of it as like a 100-metre sprint. It's like Jerzy saving the penalty was the gun to say 'you're off'. And then we were all off running after him and it began to sink in what we had done.

Me, Stevie and Ol' Big Ears (above)

I think that was at Wrexham and it was the first game after we had won the Champions League. I remember that because it was a pre-season friendly and we were getting beat 1-0 at half-time – and I came off at half-time! So we were European champions and we were losing 1-0 to Wrexham at half-time. It was brilliant to bring it out. It's just great looking at that trophy; I'd love to have it here now. I don't think there's a better trophy to look at.

Celebrating an all too rare goal (below)

This was against Kaunas. I've got a skinhead haircut as well. That doesn't look great, does it? I remember this – I think we went 1-0 down in this game, and we came back and won 3-1. It was a Champions League qualifier and I got a goal from a corner – I flicked it in. It was similar to the Aston Villa one that I got on my full debut. I haven't got many since then, have I? When you're in my position, you can't think about celebrating, you've just got to get it in the net. You don't worry about celebrations.

Captain Carra (right)

That was against CSKA Moscow. Steve couldn't play. He had travelled with us but he pulled out just before the game. That's the only trophy I have lifted as captain because Steven has always been there. So it was a nice thing for me. People don't give the Super Cup an awful lot of credit but it's a great trip for the supporters because they get to go to Monaco and watch the game. It's a great trip all around and we've won it a couple of times. To lift it was extra special.

Wembley winner (below)

That was brilliant. It was a dream of mine to play at Wembley for Liverpool. I'd been there as a kid, but to actually play there and to come on in the League Cup final was great. James, my son, got on the pitch at the end. I just got lucky in that when we were running around the pitch he was there. I wasn't sure whether he was high up in the stand or not, but he was on the lower tier, so he could get on. It's something he'll remember for the rest of his life.

It's something I'll remember for the rest of my life.
I remember taking him up to help us lift the trophy and I think he was trying to lift it before Stevie.
Typical Carragher!

Kop Quiz

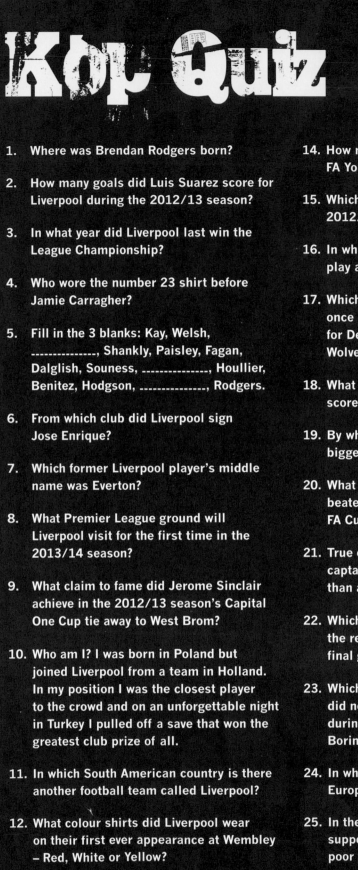

1. Where was Brendan Rodgers born?

2. How many goals did Luis Suarez score for Liverpool during the 2012/13 season?

3. In what year did Liverpool last win the League Championship?

4. Who wore the number 23 shirt before Jamie Carragher?

5. Fill in the 3 blanks: Kay, Welsh, ----------------, Shankly, Paisley, Fagan, Dalglish, Souness, ----------------, Houllier, Benitez, Hodgson, ----------------, Rodgers.

6. From which club did Liverpool sign Jose Enrique?

7. Which former Liverpool player's middle name was Everton?

8. What Premier League ground will Liverpool visit for the first time in the 2013/14 season?

9. What claim to fame did Jerome Sinclair achieve in the 2012/13 season's Capital One Cup tie away to West Brom?

10. Who am I? I was born in Poland but joined Liverpool from a team in Holland. In my position I was the closest player to the crowd and on an unforgettable night in Turkey I pulled off a save that won the greatest club prize of all.

11. In which South American country is there another football team called Liverpool?

12. What colour shirts did Liverpool wear on their first ever appearance at Wembley – Red, White or Yellow?

13. Against which club did Liverpool score the most goals in 2012/13?

14. How many times have Liverpool won the FA Youth Cup?

15. Which club eliminated Liverpool from the 2012/13 Europa League?

16. In which Australian city did Liverpool play a pre-season friendly in 2013?

17. Which current Liverpool player's uncle once played Premier League football for Derby County, Leicester City and Wolverhampton Wanderers?

18. What age was Michael Owen when he scored his first senior goal for Liverpool?

19. By what score did Liverpool record their biggest ever victory?

20. What is the nickname of the team beaten by Liverpool in the 2012/13 FA Cup third round?

21. True or False? Steven Gerrard has captained Liverpool in more games than any other player.

22. Which former Liverpool player holds the record for scoring the most FA Cup final goals?

23. Which of these three Liverpool players did not score a hat-trick for the club during 2012/13 – Luis Suarez, Fabio Borini or Daniel Sturridge?

24. In which city have Liverpool won two European Cups?

25. In the words of the popular Liverpool supporters song, what's the name of 'the poor boy sent far away from his home'?

Answers on page 61

Wordsearch

L	M	F	P	O	K	Z	W	K	W	N	V	C	K	D	J	W
L	M	V	T	K	D	G	N	T	F	Q	Q	N	T	T	L	G
P	A	G	K	Y	N	W	A	T	T	F	H	L	B	I	G	M
T	N	N	J	Q	D	Z	R	Q	R	H	G	B	V	T	W	R
M	M	F	F	M	M	G	K	C	X	T	S	E	B	R	P	T
T	Z	E	Q	I	N	B	S	F	D	R	R	W	H	F	Z	K
R	N	L	L	F	E	T	V	L	E	B	P	T	S	M	D	P
M	D	K	T	W	E	L	L	G	I	G	V	Y	J	D	H	G
K	B	K	D	R	O	Y	D	R	T	N	C	O	F	W	E	M
T	J	N	L	H	T	O	D	W	C	Z	G	H	M	A	G	R
G	V	I	B	H	R	V	D	R	N	L	N	N	H	R	E	Z
M	N	L	G	R	T	D	Y	F	K	B	Y	I	R	R	R	R
G	Z	I	M	S	H	A	N	K	L	Y	C	T	R	I	R	J
D	M	T	T	T	Z	H	R	F	Z	F	C	U	Q	O	A	T
D	M	K	J	C	B	K	T	B	M	T	M	O	B	R	R	X
F	N	L	T	T	L	C	Q	N	R	R	V	C	R	W	D	D
D	E	R	E	T	R	A	H	C	D	R	A	D	N	A	T	S

Can you find the following 15 words in the grid above?

LFC	STERLING	MIGHTY
RODGERS	KOP	YNWA
SHANKLY	REDS	LIVERBIRD
ANFIELD	COUTINHO	MELWOOD
GERRARD	STANDARD CHARTERED	WARRIOR

Answers on page 61

GOALS OF THE SEASON

Liverpool scored 98 goals in 54 games during the 2012/13 season. Here's a countdown of the best ten...

10. Nuri Sahin v West Bromwich Albion (a) Capital One Cup 3rd round: 26 September 2012

A well-worked team goal involving 11 passes resulted in Sahin tapping home to book Liverpool's place in the next round.

9. Stewart Downing v Anzhi (h) Europa League Group Phase: 25 October 2012

Cutting in from the left Downing unleashed an unstoppable shot from 25-yards out that nestled sweetly into the bottom far corner.

8. Luis Suarez v Norwich City (a) FA Barclays Premier League: 29 September 2012

The middle goal of his second successive hat-trick at Carrow Road, Suarez netted clinically with the outside of his foot just moments after spurning a gilt-edged opportunity.

7. Jordan Henderson v Newcastle United (a) FA Barclays Premier League: 27 April 2013

The Newcastle defence was cut open in a fluent forward move and Henderson was on hand to apply the finishing touch, the first of two he netted in this rout of the Magpies.

6. Glen Johnson v West Ham United (a) FA Barclays Premier League: 9 December 2012

Johnson opened the scoring against his former club, finding the top corner with a magnificent right-footed effort struck from the edge of the box.

5. Jose Enrique v Swansea City (h) FA Barclays Premier League: 17 February 2013

Coutinho, Suarez and Sturridge all combined in an eye-catching move in the left corner that saw Enrique burst into the box and stab home the third in an emphatic 5-0 win.

4. Philippe Coutinho v Queens Park Rangers (h) FA Barclays Premier League: 19 May 2013

Set up by a pass from young debutant Ibe, the little Brazilian ensured the season ended on a high with a low shot that fizzed past Robert Green and into the bottom corner.

3. Luis Suarez v Zenit St Petersburg (h) Europa League Round of 32 2nd leg: 21 February 2013

The second of Suarez's two stunning free-kicks on the night, this brilliant curling effort from 30 yards out was ultimately not enough to win the tie but it provided every Liverpool fan with a brief glimmer of hope that another famous Anfield comeback was possible.

2. Steven Gerrard v Manchester City (a) FA Barclays Premier League: 3 February 2013

Intercepting a clearance from Clichy, Gerrard controlled the ball on his chest before letting fly with a perfectly executed volley past England number one Joe Hart.

1. Luis Suarez v Newcastle United (h) FA Barclays Premier League: 4 November 2012

Liverpool's number seven at his majestic best with a sensational piece of skill that saw him expertly bring down a long forward ball and round the keeper in one seamless move before slotting into an empty net.

PLAYER PROFILES

Simon Mignolet

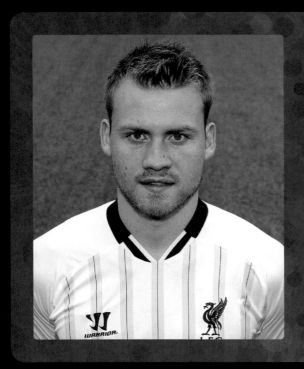

Position: **Goalkeeper**

Squad Number: **22**

Date of birth: **6 March 1988**

Birthplace: **Sint-Truiden, Belgium**

Previous clubs: **Sunderland, Coventry City (loan)**

Signed: **June 2013**

LFC Games: **0**

LFC Goals: **0**

Did You Know? **Simon is the first Belgian to play for Liverpool.**

Brad Jones

Position: **Goalkeeper**

Squad Number: **1**

Date of birth: **19 March 1982**

Birthplace: **Armadale, Australia**

Previous clubs: **Middlesbrough + loan clubs**

Signed: **August 2010**

LFC Games: **19**

LFC Goals: **0**

Did You Know? **Although born and bred in Australia, Brad's mum is originally from Liverpool.**

(Stats are correct up to the start of the 2013/14 season.)

PLAYER PROFILES

Glen Johnson

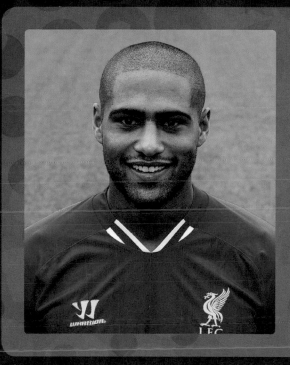

Position: Full-back

Squad Number: 2

Date of birth: 23 August 1984

Birthplace: London, England

Previous clubs: West Ham United, Millwall (loan), Chelsea, Portsmouth

Signed: June 2009

LFC Games: 142

LFC Goals: 8

Did You Know? Glen's only penalty for Liverpool was in the Carling Cup Final shoot-out against Cardiff City.

Jose Enrique

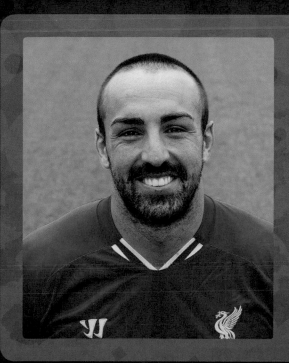

Position: Full-back

Squad Number: 3

Date of birth: 23 January 1986

Birthplace: Valencia, Spain

Previous clubs: Levante, Valencia, Celta Vigo (loan), Villarreal, Newcastle United

Signed: August 2011

LFC Games: 78

LFC Goals: 2

Did You Know? In Spain Jose's nickname was 'El Toro' (The Bull).

PLAYER PROFILES

Daniel Agger

Position: Centre-back

Squad Number: 5

Date of birth: 12 December 1984

Birthplace: Hvidovre, Denmark

Previous clubs: Brondby

Signed: January 2006

LFC Games: 209

LFC Goals: 11

Did You Know? Daniel is a keen tattoo artist and has the Latin proverb 'Mors Certa Hora Incerta' (Death is certain but its hour is not) inked on his back.

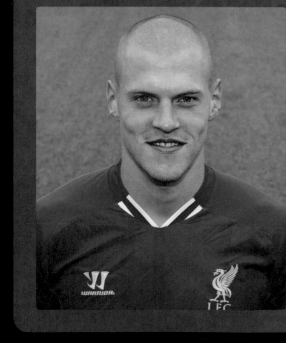

Martin Skrtel

Position: Centre-back

Squad Number: 37

Date of birth: 15 December 1984

Birthplace: Handlova, Slovakia

Previous clubs: Trencin, Zenit St Petersburg

Signed: January 2008

LFC Games: 206

LFC Goals: 9

Did You Know? Martin turned down the opportunity of a career in ice hockey to become a footballer.

PLAYER PROFILES

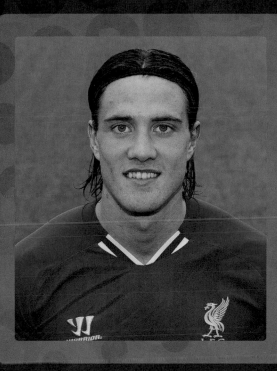

Martin Kelly

Position: Centre-back or full-back

Squad Number: 34

Date of birth: 27 April 1990

Birthplace: Whiston, England

Previous clubs: Huddersfield Town (loan)

Signed: 1997 (Academy)

LFC Games: 54

LFC Goals: 1

Did You Know? Martin's middle name is Ronald.

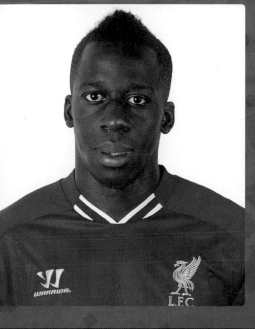

Aly Cissokho

Position: Defender

Squad Number: 20

Date of birth: 15 September 1987

Birthplace: Blois, France

Previous clubs: Gueugnon, Vitoria Setubal, Porto, Lyon, Valencia

Signed: August 2013

LFC Games: 0

LFC Goals: 0

Did You Know? Aly played against Liverpool in our games against Lyon during the 2009/10 UEFA Champions League Group Phase.

PLAYER PROFILES

Tiago Iloris

Position: Defender

Squad Number: 26

Date of birth: 26 February 1993

Birthplace: London, England

Previous clubs: Sporting Lisbon

Signed: September 2013

LFC Games: 0

LFC Goals: 0

Did You Know? Tiago played against Liverpool for Sporting in the 2011 Nextgen Series.

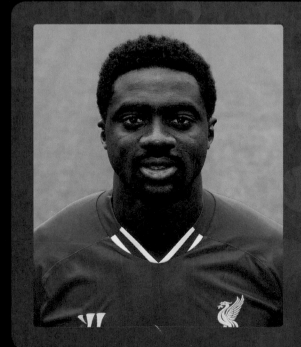

Kolo Toure

Position: Defender

Squad Number: 4

Date of birth: 19 March 1981

Birthplace: Sokoura Bouake, Ivory Coast

Previous clubs: ASEC Mimosas, Arsenal, Manchester City

Signed: June 2013

LFC Games: 0

LFC Goals: 0

Did You Know? Kolo made his Arsenal debut against Liverpool in the 2002 Community Shield.

PLAYER PROFILES

Mamadou Sakho

Position: Defender

Squad Number: 17

Date of birth: 13 February 1990

Birthplace: Paris, France

Previous clubs: Paris St Germain

Signed: September 2013

LFC Games: 0

LFC Goals: 0

Did You Know? Mamadou captained PSG when only 17, making him the youngest-ever skipper of a Ligue 1 club.

Lucas Leiva

Position: Midfield

Squad Number: 21

Date of birth: 9 January 1987

Birthplace: Dourados, Brazil

Previous clubs: Gremio

Signed: May 2007

LFC Games: 214

LFC Goals: 6

Did You Know? Lucas is the nephew of former Brazilian footballer Leivinha.

100 PLAYERS
WHO SHOOK THE KOP

A countdown of Liverpool's 100 greatest players, as voted for by visitors to the club's official website in 2013.*

100. Joey Jones (Defender 1975-78)

99. Andrew Hannah (Defender 1892-95) The club's first-ever captain, Hannah was a major player as Liverpool took their first tentative steps in the Football League

98. David Johnson (Forward 1976-82)

97. Gary Ablett (Defender 1986-92)

96. Tommy Lawrence (Goalkeeper 1962-71) Dubbed the 'Flying Pig', Lawrence was Liverpool's reliable last line of defence who won League and FA Cup honours in the sixties

95. Momo Sissoko (Midfielder 2005-08)

94. Bill Lacey (Winger 1912-24)

93. Ray Houghton (Midfielder 1987-92)

92. Alf Hanson (Winger 1933-38)

91. Bill Jones (Utility Player 1946-54)

90. Alun Evans (Forward 1968-72)

89. Matt Busby (Defender 1936-45) More famous for his time as manager of Manchester United but before then Busby was an influential pre-war captain at Anfield

88. David James (Goalkeeper 1992-99)

87. Mark Wright (Defender 1991-98)

86. Sammy Lee (Midfielder 1978-86) A passionate Liverpudlian who came through the club's youth ranks to become a pivotal member of the all-conquering Reds team of the early eighties

85. Rob Jones (Defender 1991-99)

84. Alec Lindsay (Defender 1969-77)

Players years are taken from their debut to when they left the club

83. Glenn Hysen (Defender 1989-92)

82. Bobby Graham (Forward 1964-72)

81. Peter Thompson (Winger 1963-74)

80. Donald MacKinlay (Defender 1910-29)

79. Maxi Rodriguez (Winger 2010-12)

78. Alan A'Court (Winger 1953-64) Spent most of his Anfield career in the Second Division but was still deemed good enough to represent England at the 1958 World Cup in Sweden

77. Stan Collymore (Forward 1995-97)

76. Jari Litmanen (Forward 2001-02)

75. Paul Ince (Midfielder 1997-99)

74. Jack Balmer (Forward 1935-52) A League title winner with the Reds in 1947, Balmer once scored a remarkable hat-trick of hat-tricks – an unprecedented feat which is yet to be emulated

73. Peter Crouch (Forward 2005-08)

72. Milan Baros (Forward 2002-05)

71. Yossi Benayoun (Midfielder 2007-10)

70. Geoff Strong (Utility Player 1964-70)

69. Emile Heskey (Forward 2000-04)

68. Ephraim Longworth (Defender 1910-28) The first Liverpool player to captain England, Longworth was a prominent member of the club's back-to-back title-winning team of the early twenties

67. Steve Finnan (Defender 2003-08)

66. Albert Stubbins (Forward 1946-53)

65. Craig Bellamy (Forward 2006-07 & 2011-12)

64. Chris Lawler (Defender 1963-75)

63. Jamie Redknapp (Midfielder 1991-2002)

62. Mark Lawrenson (Defender 1981-88) One of the most graceful centre-halves in Liverpool history, Lawrenson won every honour with the Reds before injury prematurely curtailed his career

61. Djibril Cisse (Forward 2004-07)

60. Jimmy Case (Midfielder 1975-81)

59.

OGDEN'S CIGARETTES.

49.

A. G. RAISBECK.

52. Gerry Byrne (Defender 1957-69) One of the toughest players to ever pull on the red shirt, Byrne famously played on in the 1965 FA Cup Final with a broken collar-bone

51. Glen Johnson (Defender 2009-present)

50. Steve Nicol (Defender 1982-95)

49. Alex Raisbeck (Defender 1898-1909) Renowned as Liverpool's first real superstar, Raisbeck captained the club to its inaugural League Championship success in 1901

48. Javier Mascherano (Midfielder 2007-10)

47. Gordon Hodgson (Forward 1926-1936) A prolific South African goalscorer who has netted more hat-tricks for the club than any other player

59. Martin Skrtel (Defender 2008-present)

58. Vladimir Smicer (Midfielder 1999-2005)

57. Craig Johnston (Midfielder 1981-88) A lovable Aussie whose never-say-die spirit endeared him to the Anfield crowd, Johnston scored Liverpool's second goal in the 1986 FA Cup Final victory over Everton

56. Bob Paisley (Defender 1946-54)

55. Patrik Berger (Midfielder 1996-2003)

54. Steve McMahon (Midfielder 1985-91)

53. Danny Murphy (Midfielder 1997-2004)

47.

46. Ronnie Whelan (Midfielder 1981-94)

45. Daniel Agger (Defender 2006-present)

44. David Fairclough (Forward 1975-83) Football's most famous 'Supersub', Fairclough's scoring exploits when coming off the bench are legendary, especially his famous strike against St Etienne in 1977

43. John Arne Riise (Defender 2001-08)

42. Terry McDermott (Midfielder 1974-82)

41. John Toshack (Forward 1970-78)

40. Ron Yeats (Defender 1961-71)

39. Elisha Scott (Goalkeeper 1913-34)

57.

38. Alan Kennedy (Defender 1978-85) Liverpool's European Cup match-winner in both 1981 and 1984, full-back Kennedy was a man for the big occasion and nicknamed 'Barney Rubble' for his foraging forward runs

37. Steve Heighway (Winger 1970-81)

36. Lucas Leiva (Midfielder 2007-present)

35. John Aldridge (Forward 1987-89)

34. Luis Garcia (Midfielder 2004-07)

33. Ian St John (Forward 1961-71) The match-winning hero of Liverpool's first FA Cup Final success in 1965, St John was a firm favourite with the Anfield crowd

32. Peter Beardsley (Forward 1987-91)

31. Gary McAllister (Midfielder 2000-02) An ageing but inspirational figure in Liverpool's unprecedented cup treble success of 2000/01

30. Phil Neal (Defender 1974-85)

29. Phil Thompson (Defender 1972-85)

28. Pepe Reina (Goalkeeper 2005-2013)

27. Jerzy Dudek (Goalkeeper 2001-07)

26. Bruce Grobbelaar (Goalkeeper 1981-94)

25. Ray Kennedy (Midfielder 1974-82)

24. Tommy Smith (Defender 1963-78)

23. Jan Molby (Midfielder 1984-96) The Great Dane who speaks with a Scouse accent. Molby was renowned for his visionary passing, long-distance shooting and expert penalty-taking

22. Dietmar Hamann (Midfielder 1999-2006)

21. Ian Callaghan (Midfielder 1960-78) Liverpool's all-time record appearance holder, Cally's remarkable career spanned 18 years, during which time the Reds rose from Second Division also-rans to Kings of Europe

20. Steve McManaman (Midfielder 1990-99)

19. Kevin Keegan (Forward 1971-77)

18. Dirk Kuyt (Forward 2006-12)

17. Ray Clemence (Goalkeeper 1970-81)

16. Roger Hunt (Forward 1959-69)

15. Emlyn Hughes (Defender 1967-79) The only man to lift two European Cups as Liverpool captain, Hughes was known as 'Crazy Horse' and his infectious enthusiasm rubbed off on all those around him

14. Michael Owen (Forward 1997-2004)

13. Xabi Alonso (Midfielder 2004-09) A Spanish midfield maestro who graced the Liverpool team for five years, helping them to Champions League and FA Cup glory in the process

12. Alan Hansen (Defender 1977-91)

11. Graeme Souness (Midfielder 1978-84)

10. Sami Hyypia (Defender 1999-2009)

9. Fernando Torres (Forward 2007-11)

8. Billy Liddell (Winger/Forward 1946-61) A brilliant Scotland international who was so good supporters renamed the team Liddellpool in his honour during the 1950s

7. John Barnes (Winger/Midfielder 1987-97) Liverpool's first high-profile black player, Barnes dazzled the crowd with his silky skills and sensational goals

6. Jamie Carragher (Defender 1997-2013)

5. Luis Suarez (Forward 2011-present)

4. Robbie Fowler (Forward 1993-2001 & 2006-07)

3. Ian Rush (Forward 1980-87 & 1988-96) Liverpool's all-time leading goalscorer, Rush fired the Reds to countless victories during two goal-laden spells at the club

2. Kenny Dalglish (Forward 1977-90)

1. Steven Gerrard (Midfielder 1998-present) Liverpool's current captain and arguably one of the best players in the world for the past decade, Stevie G is an Anfield icon who has won almost every accolade the game has to offer

HENDO @LFC

From banter to Justin Bieber, Jordan Henderson talks freely when answering a selection of questions posed by fans via the club's official Twitter account...

What would you say is your best attribute?

In my game, I tend to like to get on the ball and get my passing going – long, short and varying my passing up. I make sure I get about the pitch, closing down and pressuring people, and then getting forward into the box to try to get a goal as well. I need to improve on a lot of things; I try to improve every day when I'm training. Getting more goals from midfield is definitely one area that I've concentrated on quite a lot. Hopefully I can improve on that.

Luis Suarez's gun celebration or Daniel Sturridge's dance celebration?

I'm not sure, to be honest. I think Sturridge's dance celebration is pretty funny. Either one of them as long as they both keep scoring – I'm not really bothered.

Who has the worst banter in the squad?

The lads have got pretty good banter – we get on quite well, to be honest. Obviously some people are not that fluent in English so we might not hear the banter as much. But, to be fair, everybody has some good banter. If I had to choose one, I'd probably say Jose. I struggle sometimes with Scouse but I'm sure they struggle with my accent as well, so I think it works both ways.

Were you embarrassed when you were spotted at a Justin Bieber concert? Are you a Belieber?

Obviously not! I took my little sister. I know it's an excuse but she wanted to go for her birthday so I said I would take her. She kept reminding me so I went with my girlfriend and a couple of friends and took my little sister to watch it. It was alright, to be honest – more for kids. He has got a few good songs but I tend to keep that on the quiet.

Do you think your generation at LFC can win the league?

I think we've definitely improved over the last year and keep getting better. If we keep working hard, keep improving as players and as a team, then I definitely think we can be successful and win many trophies.

How do you keep your hair so perfect?

I put gel on my hair; the lads say I put too much on but I don't really. When it's long I've got to put a little bit more on so it doesn't go ridiculous. When it's short I don't need to do anything. The best thing to do is get your hair cut short so you don't have to do as much.

If you could take another teammate's hairstyle and model yours on that, who would you choose?

It definitely wouldn't be Jose's, he's had a different hairstyle recently. I don't think there's anyone, I'd stick with my own.

If a tree falls in a forest and nobody is around to hear it – does it make a sound?

Eh? What am I meant to say to that? Next...

What do you hope to achieve in football by the time you retire?

There are a lot of things I would like to achieve; to become very successful at Liverpool... and obviously to play for England and be successful there as well. It's just to be successful for Liverpool and England, and win as many trophies as we can.

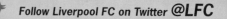

Follow Liverpool FC on Twitter @LFC

THIS IS ANFIELD

Anfield has been home to Liverpool since the club's formation in 1892 and is one of the most famous stadiums in football. Although originally the home of Everton Football Club between 1884 and 1892, it has long since become synonymous with the amazing success achieved by the Reds.

Down the years some of the game's greatest names have graced the hallowed Anfield turf and contributed to some of the most memorable matches ever played, while off the pitch the legendary Anfield atmosphere is renowned throughout the world.

Here's a selection of facts about the place we call home...

- The famous This Is Anfield sign in the players' tunnel has been in place since 1974.

- During Euro '96 Anfield played host to four games, including the quarter-final between France and Holland.

- While Wembley was being redeveloped in the early 2000s Anfield was chosen to stage several England international fixtures.

- The King and Queen of England visited Anfield for the 1921 FA Cup semi-final replay between Wolves and Cardiff.

- In 1987 Liverpool's first three home games had to be postponed due to a collapsed sewer under the Kop.

- Manchester United once played a 'home' game at Anfield. Forced to play away from Old Trafford because of crowd trouble, Anfield was the venue for their August 1971 fixture against Arsenal.

- The first ever Match of the Day show was broadcast from Anfield in August 1964, with Liverpool defeating Arsenal 3-2.

Liverpool   Football Ground
The Wrench Series No. 4480

The most famous part of Anfield is the Spion Kop. An all-seated grandstand since 1995, it was once a massive terrace that housed up to 28,000 spectators.

Anfield's current capacity is in the region of 45,000, which is broken down approximately as follows...

Main + Paddock	12200
Anfield Road Upper	2600
Anfield Road Lower	6400
Centenary Upper	4600
Centenary Lower	6800
Kop	12400

In 1989 Anfield became a shrine to the victims of Hillsborough with the pitch covered in a vast swathe of flowers.

Anfield's record attendance of 61,905 was set on 2nd February 1952 for the FA Cup fourth round tie against Wolverhampton Wanderers.

Football is not the only sport to have been played at Anfield – with British-title boxing bouts, exhibition tennis matches, rugby fixtures and the Liverpool Marathon all being staged in front of the Kop.

Anfield has also played host to many non-sporting events, including a sermon by American evangelist Billy Graham in July 1984 and, more recently, a concert by Sir Paul McCartney to tie in with the city's Capital of Culture celebrations in 2008.

PLAYER PROFILES

Jordan Henderson

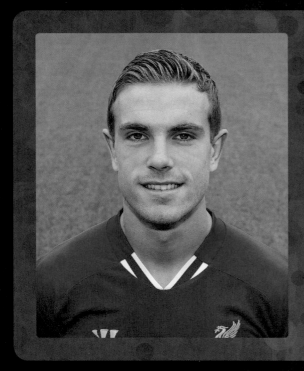

Position: **Midfield**

Squad Number: **14**

Date of birth: **17 June 1990**

Birthplace: **Sunderland, England**

Previous clubs: **Sunderland, Coventry City (loan)**

Signed: **June 2011**

LFC Games: **92**

LFC Goals: **8**

Did You Know? Jordan made his Liverpool debut against former club Sunderland on the opening day of the 2011/12 season.

Philippe Coutinho

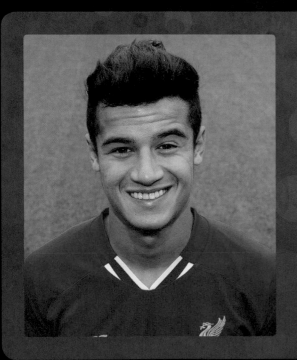

Position: **Attacking Midfield**

Squad Number: **10**

Date of birth: **12 June 1992**

Birthplace: **Rio de Janeiro, Brazil**

Previous clubs: **Vasco de Gama, Inter Milan, Espanyol (loan)**

Signed: **January 2013**

LFC Games: **13**

LFC Goals: **3**

Did You Know? Philippe was managed at Inter Milan by former Liverpool boss Rafael Benitez.

(Stats are correct up to the start of the 2013/14 season.)

PLAYER PROFILES

Steven Gerrard

Position: Midfield

Squad Number: 8

Date of birth: 30 May 1980

Birthplace: Whiston, England

Previous clubs: none

Signed: 1988 (Academy)

LFC Games: 630

LFC Goals: 159

Did You Know? Steven has now captained Liverpool more times than any other player.

Raheem Sterling

Position: Winger

Squad Number: 31

Date of birth: 8 December 1994

Birthplace: Kingston, Jamaica

Previous clubs: Queens Park Rangers

Signed: February 2012

LFC Games: 39

LFC Goals: 2

Did You Know? Raheem once scored five goals for Liverpool in a FA Youth Cup tie at home to Southend United.

PLAYER PROFILES

Joe Allen

Position: Midfield

Squad Number: 24

Date of birth: 14 March 1990

Birthplace: Carmarthen, Wales

Previous clubs: Swansea City

Signed: August 2012

LFC Games: 37

LFC Goals: 2

Did You Know? Joe represented Team GB in the 2012 Olympics.

Luis Alberto

Position: Forward

Squad Number: 6

Date of birth: 28 September 1992

Birthplace: San Jose Del Valle, Spain

Previous clubs: Sevilla, Barcelona B (loan)

Signed: June 2013

LFC Games: 0

LFC Goals: 0

Did You Know? Luis has represented Spain at U18, U19 and U21 level.

PLAYER PROFILES

Iago Aspas

Position: Forward

Squad Number: 9

Date of birth: 1 August 1987

Birthplace: Moana, Spain

Previous clubs: Celta Vigo, Rapido Bouzas (loan)

Signed: June 2013

LFC Games: 0

LFC Goals: 0

Did You Know? During his time at Celta Vigo Iago worked with former Liverpool coach Paco Herrera.

Victor Moses

Position: Forward

Squad Number: 12

Date of birth: 12 December 1990

Birthplace: Lagos, Nigeria

Previous clubs: Crystal Palace, Wigan Athletic, Chelsea

Signed: September 2013

LFC Games: 0

LFC Goals: 0

Did You Know? Although born in Nigeria Victor moved to England when he was 11.

PLAYER PROFILES

Luis Suarez

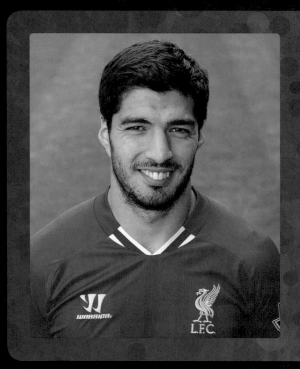

Position: Forward

Squad Number: 7

Date of birth: 24 January 1987

Birthplace: Salto, Uruguay

Previous clubs: Nacional, Groningen, Ajax

Signed: January 2011

LFC Games: 96

LFC Goals: 51

Did You Know? Luis was named player of the tournament when Uruguay won the Copa America in 2011.

Daniel Sturridge

Position: Forward

Squad Number: 15

Date of birth: 1 September 1989

Birthplace: Birmingham, England

Previous clubs: Manchester City, Bolton Wanderers (loan), Chelsea

Signed: January 2013

LFC Games: 16

LFC Goals: 11

Did You Know? Daniel was on the losing side for Manchester City against Liverpool in the 2006 FA Youth Cup Final.

Picture Quiz

1. Name the country

CLUE: It was Brendan Rodgers' first competitive game as Liverpool manager.

2. Name the trophy

CLUE: It has since changed names.

3. Name the stadium

CLUE: It was a pretty successful hunting ground for Liverpool in the 2000s.

4. Name The Year

CLUE: It was one of double delight for the Reds.

5. Can you name the 4 players in each of the montages below?

CLUE: All four are former players.

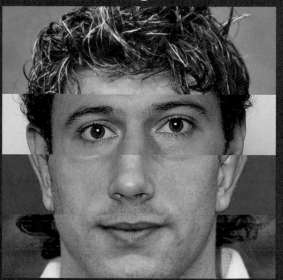

CLUE: Three are former players, one is current.

Answers on page 61

LIVERPOOL FC
FOUNDATION
HOPE IN YOUR HEART

For over 20 years Liverpool FC has been working in the community. All projects promote social inclusion, football for all and encourage health and wellbeing in people of all ages and abilities from a diverse range of backgrounds. Our goal is to provide opportunities that inspire positive change and help build better futures for people of all ages.

MEN'S HEALTH

Developed in 2005 in response to the high levels of poor health in the local community we aim to tackle issues such as poor diet, obesity, heart disease, low physical activity levels and cancer prevention as well as mental health and wellbeing. Through an extensive partnership agreement with Liverpool Clinical Commissioning Group our programme offers a wide range of activities to suit everyone and has engaged over 4500 men since it began.

FOOTBALL FOR ALL

Football is at the heart of what we do. One of our key programmes is our Disability and Equality Football Coaching and earlier this year the Foundation was proud to open its second centre in the Wirral. Lucas Leiva officially opened the centre and has made several visits to our programmes, meeting participants and getting involved with the programme activities.

YOUTH SKILLS

The Foundation Youth Skills Programme is currently being developed with a range of partners. This exciting new project will pilot throughout a range of secondary schools from September 2013. The overall aim of the programme is to equip young people for life, work and citizenship and reduce the risks of disengagement from education through active learning in the community.

ON THE BALL

On the Ball is a project that started in October 2012; working intensively with All Saints Catholic Primary, Anfield Infants and Anfield Juniors, the aim is to have a positive impact in the areas of attendance, attainment, health and wellbeing and confidence. Working closely with the Club's mascot, Mighty Red, on the new attendance and punctuality scheme, we have already seen an increase in attendance.

INTERNATIONAL

Our international programme provides unique opportunities to a diverse range of individuals and community groups. By providing professional coaching clinics, educational workshops and with support from our partners globally, we aim to establish a legacy in every country we visit. This year the Foundation team have delivered football coaching in several international locations including Qatar, South Africa, the US and Cyprus.

To find out more about our programmes visit www.liverpoolfc.com/foundation and follow us on twitter @LFCFoundation

They have been the face of Liverpool's official television channel since it launched six years ago. Here, Claire Rourke and Matt Critchley tell us a bit more about their roles at LFC TV...

What has been your most memorable moment while working for the channel?

CR: There have been so many moments that I savour; I get the opportunity to be at the forefront of the channel's coverage for the biggest events. I loved hosting the 2012 Carling Cup final broadcast alongside Matt and the fact that we won made everything all the more special. I am also fortunate to go on the pre season tours which are always memorable.

MC: There have been so many. From the early days and our first shows to some great European trips to the likes of Milan and Madrid to see the Reds win in some of the most iconic stadiums on the continent. Presenting our live coverage of the Hillsborough Truth Day was perhaps my proudest moment with the station but I must mention the live build-up programmes we put together ahead of the two Wembley Finals in 2012. They were both very special.

What is the hardest part of the job?

CR: Throughout the past six years there have been some testing moments with the takeovers and changing of managers, but I think the hardest part of the job is having the responsibility to deliver something to the supporters that they can be proud of.

MC: Certain shows can be demanding – people probably don't realise exactly what it's like to be a TV presenter during a live programme when you are talking to guests, your producer, director and PA are talking to you down your ear and you have to be aware of where you are, where you've been and where you're going next. But it's so much fun to do. When we get it right it really is one of the best jobs in the world.

Are there any particular shows you enjoy working on most?

CR: We have the opportunity to work on such a variety of shows, but I'd have to say the match days are probably the most enjoyable as that's what the entire week is geared towards. But I also work in 'Kop Kids' which is great fun and something different on the channel.

MC: The live matchday programmes have been fantastic to work on but I always enjoy the 'Sixty Minutes With' programme, when a Liverpool legend comes into the studio to talk through his career. To share a sofa with some of the greats of our club is an honour in itself and it's fantastic when you hear stories that you weren't expecting.

Describe your dream scenario as an LFC TV presenter.

CR: The dream scenario for me would be hosting the coverage on the final day of a season when Liverpool win the league. I can't begin to imagine what the celebrations would be like and to be involved in them would be incredible.

MC: Simple. Broadcasting live from Wembley as the Reds win the European Cup for a sixth time. It will happen!

Who would you interview from Liverpool's history, and why?

CR: The obvious person for me has to be Bill Shankly. I'd love to know his thoughts on the way football has changed over the years and what he would think about the media's role in today's game. I imagine I'd just be hanging on his every word.

MC: I would actually go for Sir Bob Paisley as he was a very different character indeed and yet still the only man to win three European Cups as a manager – and all in five years. Speak to those who played under him and they'll tell you he was a quiet, shy and very un-Shankly-like type of man. So how did he achieve so much? What did he say and how did he do it? I'd love to find out.

What advice would you give to any youngsters with aspirations of pursuing a career as a football presenter?

CR: Get plenty of work experience – it really is the best way to learn. I spent a lot of time chasing work placements. The experience you get is invaluable.

MC: Be prepared to put the work in, be humble, get your opportunity in TV if you can and then just take it from there. It's not the best paid job in the world, they're not the best working hours in the world but, if you can't be a footballer, then this is the best job in the world, without a doubt.

The Messiah addresses his vast army of fans on the steps of St Georges Hall.

SHANKLY 100

Bill Shankly remains the most iconic manager in Liverpool history. Other managers may have won more in terms of silverware but no-one inspired a transformation in the club's fortunes like Shanks.

Recruited from Huddersfield Town in 1959, he succeeded Phil Taylor as Liverpool manager with the task of restoring the club's top-flight status that had been surrendered five years previously.

Success didn't come overnight but within three years the Reds were back in Division One and would soon be champions. Another title followed two years later, while sandwiched in-between was an unforgettable first FA Cup triumph.

He led the Reds into Europe and put the pride back into supporting the club. Worshipped by Kopites who hung on his every word, Shankly was viewed as the Messiah.

When that great team of the sixties began to age he built another – one that would achieve an unprecedented League and UEFA Cup double in 1973.

The great man continues to oversee life at Anfield. This statue of him was erected outside the Kop in 1999.

Commissioned and donated by

'Liverbird On My Chest'... a proud Shankly leads his team out at Wembley for the 1971 FA Cup Final against Arsenal.

More success in the FA Cup followed but in July 1974 he suddenly announced his resignation. To say the football world was stunned would be an understatement. Liverpool had lost the services of the game's most charismatic manager but he had laid the foundations for all that followed.

He passed away in 1981 but his achievements at Anfield have never been forgotten. In September 2013 Bill Shankly would have celebrated his 100th birthday and so we take this opportunity to salute the club's modern day founding father...

Fact-file

BORN: Glenbuck, Scotland, 2nd September 1913

PLAYING CAREER: Carlisle United, Preston North End, Scotland

MANAGEMENT CAREER: Carlisle United, Grimsby Town, Workington, Huddersfield Town, Liverpool

Roll of Honour as Liverpool Manager

- Second Division Championship 1961/62
- First Division Championship 1963/64
- FA Cup 1965
- First Division Championship 1965/66
- First Division Championship 1972/73
- UEFA Cup 1973
- Manager of the Year 1973
- FA Cup 1974

Handing over the reins... Shankly wishes his reluctant successor Bob Paisley the best of luck.

His first team of Champions – Shankly and the 1963-64 title-winners.

He Made The People Happy... a fan wraps a scarf around his hero's neck as Shankly bows out of Wembley following the 1974 Charity Shield.

'Outside the Shankly Gates'... a young boy stands and stares at the memory of Bill Shankly.

Shankly delivers his last piece of silverware to the Liverpool supporters on the 1974 FA Cup winners homecoming parade.

As well as the remarkable success his teams achieved on the pitch, Bill Shankly was renowned for his quick-witted observations and humorous one-liners off it.

Here are ten of his most memorable...

"Some people believe football is a matter of life and death. I am very disappointed with that attitude. I can assure you it is much, much more important than that."

"If you are first you are first. If you are second you are nothing."

"Liverpool was made for me and I was made for Liverpool."

"I was only in the game for the love of football – and I wanted to bring back happiness to the people of Liverpool."

"If Everton were playing at the bottom of the garden, I'd pull the curtains."

"Fire in your belly comes from pride and passion in wearing the red shirt. We don't need to motivate players because each of them is responsible for the performance of the team as a whole. The status of Liverpool's players keeps them motivated."

"Football is a simple game based on the giving and taking of passes, of controlling the ball and of making yourself available to receive a pass. It is terribly simple."

"At a football club there's a holy trinity – the players, the manager and the supporters. Directors don't come into it. They are only there to sign the cheques."

"I'm just one of the people who stands on the Kop. They think the same as I do, and I think the same as they do. It's a kind of marriage of people who like each other."

"Above all, I would like to be remembered as a man who was selfless, who strove and worried so that others could share the glory, and who built up a family of people who could hold their heads up high and say... WE ARE LIVERPOOL."

LIVERPOOL LADIES

Founder members of the recently launched FA Women's Super League, Liverpool Ladies have made great strides this past year.

Managed by ex-Chelsea and Millwall boss Matt Beard and containing star names such as Fara Williams, Whitney Engen, Amanda Da Costa and Louise Fors, our ladies in Red are now firmly established as one of the country's top sides.

Originally formed as Newton Ladies in 1989, the club changed its name to Knowsley Women's Football Club in 1991 before beginning its association with Liverpool Football Club in 1994.

To coincide with the inaugural FA WSL season in 2013 it was announced that the Ladies team would become a fully integrated operation within LFC and in April they were invited along to Melwood by Brendan Rodgers for a special training sessions alongside the first team.

Home games are staged at the 13,000 capacity Halton stadium and future talent is nurtured at the Ladies Centre of Excellence which runs teams at U9, U11, U13, U15 and U17 level.

Liverpool Ladies are one of eight teams in the FA Women's Super League, the others being Arsenal Ladies, Birmingham City Ladies, Bristol Academy Women, Chelsea Ladies, Doncaster Rovers Belles, Everton Ladies and Lincoln Ladies.

For more information about the LFC Ladies and details of when games are played visit www.liverpoolladiesfc.com

Honours

FA WPL Northern
Winners: 2004, 2007, 2010

FA Cup
Runners up: 1994,1995,1996

League Cup
Runners up: 1993

Keele Classic
Winners: 2010

Preston Tournament
Winners: 2010

Young Guns

The 2012/13 campaign was another highly productive one for Liverpool's Academy system.

In recent years we've seen the likes of Martin Kelly, Jay Spearing, Jack Robinson, Jon Flanagan and Raheem Sterling all rise through the ranks of the club's Kirkby-based youth complex and last season offered more conclusive proof that the conveyor belt is continuing to churn out potential stars of the future.

Here we turn the focus on a selection of other highly promising starlets who have all followed in the footsteps of those listed above by breaking into the first team squad during the course of the past season...

Conor Coady

Born: *Warrington, 25 February 1993*

A commanding central midfielder who has also operated in the centre of defence, Coady is captain of Liverpool Under-21s and was handed a well-deserved first team debut in November 2012 away to Anzhi in the Europa League. Later in the season he came on as a late substitute to make his Premier League bow in Liverpool's 3-1 away win at Fulham. Coady's association with the Reds began when he was just eight and he has since also skippered England Under-17s to glory in the 2010 European Championships. In order to gain more first team experience he was loaned out to League One side Sheffield United in readiness for the 2013/14 season.

Andre Wisdom

Born: *Leeds, 9 May 1993*

Powerful defender Wisdom was snapped up by the Reds from Bradford City when he was only 14 years of age and, after progressing through the youth ranks at the Academy, the club's judgement has so far been proved correct. An England youth international and under-21 international, he was originally handed a first-team squad number during Roy Hodgson's tenure as manager but had to wait until September 2012 before making his debut. This came in a match away to Young Boy Berne in the Europa League, a game in which he also netted his first goal. Wisdom was rewarded with a new long-term contract in January 2013 and ended last season with an impressive 19 senior starts under his belt.

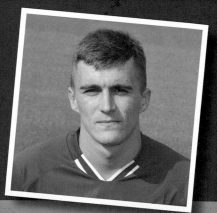

Adam Morgan

Born: *Liverpool, 21 April 1994*

A forward from Halewood in Liverpool, Morgan has been at the club since he was a schoolboy and proved himself as a prolific goalscorer at youth level. His fine form was rewarded with a call-up to the squad for the 2012 summer tour of North America and he made his mark by scoring in the 1-1 draw against Toronto. This was quickly followed up by a competitive first team debut in August for the second leg of the Europa League play-off at home to Hearts, in which he had a goal disallowed.

Jerome Sinclair

Born: *Birmingham, 20 September 1996*

Liverpool's youngest-ever first team debutant, Sinclair made history when coming off the bench in the Capital One Cup tie away to West Brom in September 2012. At just 16 years and six days old he smashed the previous record when coming on in the 81st minute of the Reds' 2-1 victory. The Birmingham-born forward joined Liverpool's Academy as a 14-year old in 2011 and is an England Under-17 international.

Jordan Ibe

Born: *London, 8 December 1995*

Snapped up from Wycombe Wanderers at the end of 2011, Ibe is an exciting front-man who is equally adept at playing through the middle or out wide. He travelled with the senior squad to North America during the summer of 2012 and was voted the 2012/13 Academy Player of the Year but the undoubted highlight of his career so far came on the final day of the 2012/13 campaign when he was handed his competitive first team debut. Wearing the number 44 shirt he made an instant impression at Anfield with a lively performance against Queens Park Rangers that included an assist for Philippe Coutinho's winning goal.

Samed Yesil

Born: *Dusseldorf, 25 May 1994*

Liverpool's capture of Yesil from Bayer Leverkusen during the summer of 2012 was considered quite a coup. The highly-rated striker from Germany had shot to prominence in the previous year's Under-17 World Cup and his signature was much sought after. Within a month of his arrival at Anfield he was pitched into his first team debut for the Capital One Cup tie away to West Brom and made one further appearance before an untimely injury prematurely curtailed his season.

Lloyd Jones

Born: *Plymouth, 7 October 1995*

A place among the substitutes for Liverpool's trip to Fulham in May 2013 was a just reward for the impressive progress made by Jones following his arrival from Plymouth two years previously. After starting out in the Liverpool Under-16 side Jones has since established himself in the Under-18 set-up and also broke into the Under-21s. A powerful and cultured centre-back who's dominant in the air, he was born in England but plays for Wales at youth level.

2012/13 SEASON IN STATS...

APPEARANCES

	PL	FA	LC	EL	Total
Steven Gerrard	36	1	1	8	46
Stewart Downing	29	2	2	12	45
Luis Suarez	33	2	1	8	44
Jordan Henderson	30	2	2	10	44
Glen Johnson	36	0	0	7	43
Daniel Agger	35	0	0	4	39
Pepe Reina	31	0	0	8	39
Jamie Carragher	24	1	2	11	38
Joe Allen	27	2	1	7	37
Raheem Sterling	24	1	1	10	36
Jose Enrique	29	0	0	6	35
Martin Skrtel	25	1	0	7	33
Jonjo Shelvey	19	2	1	10	32
Lucas Leiva	26	1	0	4	31
Suso	14	1	1	4	20
Fabio Borini	13	1	0	6	20
Andre Wisdom	12	2	1	4	19
Daniel Sturridge	14	2	0	0	16
Brad Jones	7	2	2	4	15
Philippe Coutinho	13	0	0	0	13
Nuri Sahin	7	0	1	4	12
Sebastian Coates	5	2	2	3	12
Oussama Assaidi	4	0	2	6	12
Joe Cole	6	0	1	3	10
Martin Kelly	4	0	0	3	7
Jack Robinson	0	2	2	2	6
Jay Spearing	0	0	0	3	3
Dani Pacheco	0	0	1	2	3
Adam Morgan	0	0	0	3	3
Jon Flanagan	0	1	0	1	2
Conor Coady	1	0	0	1	2
Charlie Adam	0	0	0	2	2
Andy Carroll	2	0	0	0	2
Samed Yesil	0	0	2	0	2
Jordon Ibe	1	0	0	0	1
Jerome Sinclair	0	0	1	0	1

BEST PASSER (Premier League only)

1. *Steven Gerrard – 2,053 successful passes*
2. *Daniel Agger – 1,552 successful passes*
3. *Glen Johnson – 1,427 successful passes*

BEST TACKLER (Premier League only)

1. *Lucas Leiva – 90 successful tackles*
2. *Glen Johnson – 73 successful tackles*
3. *Steven Gerrard – 66 successful tackles*

MOST ASSISTS (Premier League only)

1. *Steven Gerrard – 9*
2. *Luis Suarez, Stewart Downing & Philippe Coutinho – 5*
3. *Jordan Henderson, Jose Enrique & Glen Johnson – 4*

Liverpool scored a total of 98 goals during the 2012/13 season, averaging 1.81 goals per game.

In terms of competition the goals were spread out as follows...

Premier League – 71
Europa League –20
FA Cup – 4
League Cup – 3

The Reds were more prolific in the second half of games scoring 56 times, as opposed to 42 in the first half.

The most popular time for Liverpool to score a goal (22 times) was between 46 and 60 minutes.

They scored 2 injury time goals: at home to Fulham, 90+3, home to Chelsea 90+7.

Liverpool finished with a goal difference of +28 – the club's best since 2008/09.

The 38 league goals Liverpool scored away from home was the most since the club's last title-winning season of 1989/90.

18 different players were on the score-sheet for Liverpool in 2012/13, with leading scorer Luis Suarez the first Liverpool player to register 30 goals in a season since Fernando Torres in 2007/08.

GOALSCORERS

	PL	FA	LC	EL	Total
Luis Suarez	23	1	2	4	30
Daniel Sturridge	10	0	1	0	11
Steven Gerrard	9	0	0	1	10
Own goals	4	0	0	2	6
Jordan Henderson	5	0	0	1	6
Stewart Downing	3	0	0	2	5
Jonjo Shelvey	1	0	0	4	5
Daniel Agger	3	0	0	0	3
Nuri Sahin	1	2	0	0	3
Philippe Coutinho	3	0	0	0	3
Raheem Sterling	2	0	0	0	2
Fabio Borini	1	0	0	1	2
Joe Allen	0	0	1	1	2
Martin Skrtel	2	0	0	0	2
Joe Cole	1	0	0	1	2
Glen Johnson	1	0	0	1	2
Jose Enrique	2	0	0	0	2
Sebastian Coates	0	0	0	1	1
Andre Wisdom	0	0	0	1	1

DEBUTANTS

The following 13 players made their Liverpool first team debuts during 2012/13...

Fabio Borini – 2 August 2012 v FC Gomel (a)

Joe Allen – 18 August 2012 v West Bromwich Albion (a)

Adam Morgan – 23 August 2012 v Hearts (h)

Nuri Sahin – 2 September 2012 v Arsenal (h)

Oussama Assaidi – 20 September 2012 v Young Boys (a)

Suso – 20 September 2012 v Young Boys (a)

Andre Wisdom – 20 September 2012 v Young Boys (a)

Samed Yesil – 26 September 2012 v West Bromwich Albion (a)

Jerome Sinclair – 26 September 2012 v West Bromwich Albion (a)

Conor Coady – 8 November 2012 v FC Anzhi (a)

Daniel Sturridge – 6 January 2013 v Mansfield Town (a)

Philippe Coutinho – 11 February 2013 v West Bromwich Albion (h)

Jordon Ibe – 19 May 2013 v Queens Park Rangers (h)

PENALTIES

Steven Gerrard v Stoke City (a) – Scored

Steven Gerrard v West Bromwich Albion (h) – Missed

Daniel Sturridge v Swansea City (h) – Scored

Steven Gerrard v Swansea City (h) – Scored

Steven Gerrard v Tottenham Hotspur (h) – Scored

Steven Gerrard v Aston Villa (a) – Scored

HAT-TRICKS

Luis Suarez v Norwich City (a)

Luis Suarez v Wigan Athletic (a)

Daniel Sturridge v Fulham (a)

OWN GOALS

(by opposition players)

Andy Webster – Heart of Midlothian (a)

Juhani Ojala – Young Boys (a)

Leon Barnett – Norwich City (a)

Leighton Baines – Everton (a)

Gareth Bale – Tottenham Hotspur (a)

Ryan Bennett – Norwich City (h)

(by Liverpool players)

Sebastian Coates – Udinese (h)

Steven Gerrard – West Ham United (a)

CLEAN SHEETS

Liverpool recorded 21 clean sheets throughout 2012/13...

Pepe Reina – 17 (in 39 games)

Brad Jones – 4 (in 15 games)

Liverpool's highest league position during 2012/13 was 6th.

Liverpool's lowest league position during 2012/13 was 18th, after matches 1, 3 and 5.

Liverpool's final Premier League finishing position was 7th.

Liverpool's final Premier League points tally of 61 was the club's best since 2009/10.

Liverpool's biggest win was 6-0 away to Newcastle United.

Liverpool's heaviest defeat was 0-3 away to West Bromwich Albion.

INSIDE
MELWOOD

The club photographer takes us through the gates of the training ground to capture this great selection of snaps as the players are put through their paces.

LFC TOUR 2013

JAKARTA | MELBOURNE | BANGKOK

PRESENTED BY

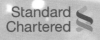

Standard
Chartered

In July 2013 Liverpool's players embarked on what was to be the most successful pre-season tour in the club's history – a twenty one and a half thousand mile round trek to three cities, in three different countries, to play three games watched by two hundred and twenty four thousand fanatical supporters!

It was a trip that included ground-breaking first-ever visits to Indonesia and Australia as well as Thailand and it brought the world's biggest footballing family closer to some of its long-lost relatives. The reception the team received in Jakarta, Melbourne and Bangkok was truly out of this world, and for all those who made the trip the memories will live forever.

Not only that, it was an ideal opportunity to prepare for the 2013/14 FA Barclays Premier League campaign with three wins out of three, seven goals scored and none conceded.

Here are some of the highlights...

Win a signed football shirt!

Answer the following question correctly and you could win a Liverpool FC shirt signed by a first team player.

On 26th September 2012 Liverpool FC's youngest-ever player made his first-team debut at 16 years and 6 days of age, in a League Cup match against West Bromich Albion. Choose the correct player from the following for your chance to win.

a. Jerome Sinclair   b. Andre Wisdom   c. Jon Flanagan

Entry is by email only. One entry only per contestant. Please enter **SHIRT** followed by either **A**, **B** or **C** in the subject line of an email, and send to: **frontdesk@grangecommunications.co.uk** by Thursday March 27, 2014.

Terms and Conditions

1) The closing date for this competition is Thursday March 27, 2014 at 4pm. Entries received after that time will not be counted.

2) Information on how to enter and on the prizes form part of these conditions.

3) Entry is open in the UK to those aged 18 years or over. This competition is not open to employees or their relatives of Liverpool FC. Any such entries will be invalid.

4) The start date for entries is 1st October 2013 at 4pm.

5) Entries must be strictly in accordance with these terms and conditions. Any entry not in strict accordance with these terms and conditions will be deemed to be invalid and no prizes will be awarded in respect of such entry. By entering, all entrants will be deemed to accept these rules.

6) One (1) lucky winner will win a 2013/14 season signed football shirt.

7) The prize is non transferable and no cash alternative will be offered. Entry is by email only. One entry only per contestant. Please enter SHIRT followed by either A, B or C in the subject line of an email, and send to: frontdesk@grangecommunications. co.uk by Thursday March 27, 2014.

8) The winner will be picked at random. The winner will be contacted within 24 hours of the closing date. Details of the winners can be requested after this time from the address below.

9) Entries must not be sent in through agents or third parties. No responsibility can be accepted for lost, delayed, incomplete, or for electronic entries or winning notifications that are not received or delivered. Any such entries will be deemed void.

10) The winners shall have 72 hours to claim their prize once initial contact has been made by the Promoter. Failure to respond may result in forfeiture of the prize.

11) The Promoter will not contact Entrants with any marketing information.

12) The Promoter reserves the right to withdraw or amend the promotion as necessary due to circumstances outside its reasonable control. The Promoter's decision on all matters is final and no correspondence will be entered into.

13) The Promoter (or any third party nominated by the Promoter) may use the winner's name and image and their comments relating to the prize for future promotional, marketing and publicity purposes in any media worldwide without notice or without any fee being paid.

14) Liverpool Football Club's decision is final: no correspondence will be entered in to. Except in respect of death or personal injury resulting from any negligence of the Club, neither The Liverpool Football Club nor any of its officers, employees or agents shall be responsible for (whether in tort, contract or otherwise):

(i) any loss, damage or injury to you and/or any guest or to any property belonging to you or any guest in connection with this competition and/or the prize, resulting from any cause whatsoever;

(ii) for any loss of profit, loss of use, loss of opportunity or any indirect, economic or consequential losses whatsoever.

15) This competition shall be governed by English law.

16) Promoter: Grange Communications Ltd., 22 Great King Street, Edinburgh EH3 6QH

Quiz Answers

Kop Quiz (page 24)

1. Carnlough, Northern Ireland
2. 30
3. 1990
4. Robbie Fowler
5. Taylor, Evans, Dalglish
6. Newcastle United
7. Mark Walters
8. Cardiff City Stadium
9. He became Liverpool's youngest-ever player
10. Jerzy Dudek
11. Uruguay
12. White
13. Norwich City (10)
14. Three
15. Zenit St Petersburg
16. Melbourne
17. Daniel Sturridge
18. 17
19. 11-0
20. The Stags
21. True
22. Ian Rush
23. Fabio Borini
24. Rome
25. Tommy

Wordsearch (page 25)

L	M	F	P	O	K	Z	W	K	W	N	V	C	K	D	J	W
L	M	V	T	K	D	G	N	T	F	Q	Q	N	T	T	L	G
P	A	G	K	Y	N	W	A	T	T	F	H	L	B	I	G	M
T	N	N	J	Q	D	Z	R	Q	R	H	G	B	V	T	W	R
M	M	F	F	M	M	G	K	C	X	T	S	E	B	R	P	T
T	Z	E	Q	I	N	B	S	F	D	R	R	W	H	F	Z	K
R	N	L	L	F	E	T	V	L	E	B	P	T	S	M	D	P
M	D	K	T	W	E	L	L	G	I	G	V	Y	J	D	H	G
K	B	K	D	R	O	Y	D	R	T	N	C	O	F	W	E	M
T	J	N	L	H	T	O	D	W	C	Z	G	H	M	A	G	R
G	V	I	B	H	R	V	D	R	N	L	N	N	H	R	E	Z
M	N	L	G	R	T	D	Y	F	K	B	Y	I	R	R	R	R
G	Z	I	M	S	H	A	N	K	L	Y	C	T	R	I	R	J
D	M	T	T	T	Z	H	R	F	Z	F	C	U	Q	O	A	T
D	M	K	J	C	B	K	T	B	M	T	M	O	B	R	R	X
F	N	L	T	T	L	C	Q	N	R	R	V	C	R	W	D	D
D	E	R	E	T	R	A	H	C	D	R	A	D	N	A	T	S

Picture Quiz (page 47)

1. Name the country: Belarus
2. Name the trophy: UEFA Cup
3. Name the stadium: Millennium (Cardiff)
4. Name the year: 1986
5. Name the players
   (1): Jamie Carragher, Robbie Fowler, Patrik Berger, Stig Inge Bjornebye
   (2): Luis Garcia, Javier Mascherano, Jordan Henderson, Jason McAteer

MEET MIGHTY RED!

I have 7 spikes on each arm, plus 4 spikes on my tail = 18. This is how many times LFC have won the League.

I have two wristbands, one on each wrist. One says **Mighty Red** and the other says **Y.N.W.A.** which stands for **'You'll Never Walk Alone'.**

I have 5 spikes on my head and neck – one for each time LFC has won the European Cup.

Mighty Red

Job: Liverpool FC Official Mascot

Age: 8

School: St Anfield Junior School

Lives: Liverpool

Nickname: Mighty

Favourite drink: Milk

Favourite footie position: Striker

Favourite song: You'll Never Walk Alone

Pet: Fred the Iguana

Hobbies: Footie, supporting LFC, singing at LFC matches, video games, playing pranks

Dislikes: Sitting still, too much homework and sprouts